Aylesworth
Servants of the devil

SERVANTS OF THE DEVIL

To my daughter, Carol,
who like all children everywhere
knows as much about witchcraft as I do

ADDISON-WESLEY

THOMAS G. AYLESWORTH

Servants of the evil

An Addisonian Press Book

Books by Thomas G. Aylesworth

Servants of the Devil
Werewolves and Other Monsters
Vampires and Other Ghosts
The Alchemists: Magic Into Science

Addison-Wesley Publishing Company, Inc.
Reading, Massachusetts 01867
Library of Congress Catalog Card Number 73–118996
Printed in the United States of America

ISBN: 0–201–00145–4
EFGHIJ–WZ–7987

CONTENTS

Introduction 9

1 In The Beginning 11

2 Joining the Group 23

3 Ceremonies and Feasts 45

4 The Sacrifice and Other Sports 62

5 Witch Power 71

6 Hunting Witches 83

7 The Black Mass 100

8 White Witches 106

9 Science and Witchcraft 111

Acknowledgements 121

Index 123

A Scottish print,
dating from 1591,
of the Devil preaching
to the witches
of North Berwick Kirk.

INTRODUCTION/ Probably only about fifty per cent of the "facts" in this book are true. My only wish is that I knew which fifty per cent they were. The problem is that most of the items of information presented here come from the reports of people who talked to witches (who may or may not have been real witches) or from people who thought that they themselves were witches (and who may have been either witches or mental patients).

The question arises, "Are there such things as witches?" The answer must be, "Of course there are." Although most of the people who were tortured and executed on charges of witchcraft were probably really not witches, there are hundreds of people, even today, who maintain that they themselves are witches. Who am I to argue, especially considering the many things that modern science still does not know about extrasensory perception, psychiatry, the inner workings of the human mind, or even what makes a person accident-prone.

There are many problems involved in writing a book about witchcraft. The biggest one is: whose theories do we accept? There are a huge number of conflicting ideas on the subject, and a writer who has never been a witch must pick and choose. One cannot prove that there was no system of covens of witches in the Middle Ages. We really do not know whether the witches danced before or after the banquet at the Sabbat. No one is sure that witches ever met at functions called Esbats. All that I can say is, you pay your money and you take your choice. When it comes to witchcraft, no one knows for sure. That is, unless he happens to have a special pipeline to some demon or other.

Thomas G. Aylesworth
Stamford, Connecticut
Walpurgis Night, 1969

ONE / IN THE BEGINNING / What is a witch?

In these modern times, when we try to believe that we are guided by common sense, our knowledge of these strange creatures seems to be a little vague.

Perhaps we think of the three witches in *Macbeth.* Shakespeare (who, according to some historians, accepted witchcraft as a fact) has them preparing a delicious brew consisting of:

Eye of newt and toe of frog,
Wool of bat and tongue of dog,
Adder's fork and blind-worm's sting,
Lizard's leg and howlet's wing . . .
Nose of Turk and Tartar's lips,
Finger of birth-strangled babe . . .
For the ingredients of our cauldron.

Perhaps we remember the good and evil witches in *The Wizard of Oz.* Both of these were able to do all sorts of magic tricks, but the good witch, fortunately for Dorothy, was more powerful than the bad witch.

Or we may recall the Brothers Grimm and their frightening old crone who made life so difficult for Hansel and Gretel. In the opera, *Hansel and Gretel,* she cheers up the two children with:

First with Gretel I'll begin,
Off you, dear Gretel, I will dine.
You're so tender, plump, and good,
Just the thing for witch's food.

But one of the best descriptions of a witch was written in the 1500's by an English lawyer named William West:

> A witch or hag is she which being deluded by a league made with the Devil through his persuasion, inspiration, and juggling, thinketh she can design what manner of evil things soever, either by thought or imprecation, as to shake the air with lightnings and thunder, to cause hail and tempests, to remove green corn or trees to another place, to be carried of her familiar (which hath taken upon him the deceitful shape of a goat, swine, or calf, etc.) into some mountain far distant, in a wonderful short space of time, and sometimes to fly upon a staff or fork, or some other instrument, and to spend all the night after with her sweetheart, in playing, sporting, banqueting, dancing, dalliance, and divers other devilish

lusts and lewd disports, and to show a thousand such monstrous mockeries.

That's quite a mouthful.

All of these examples, of course, are caricatures of the real thing. The *real* thing? Well, it may be that there are no such things as witches, but throughout the history of man's life upon this planet, there have been so many people who claimed that they were witches and so many people who believed them, that we ought to investigate the subject before we say that they do not exist.

Man seems to pride himself on the belief that, the more modern he is, the less likely he is to fear the supernatural. It may seem strange, then, to find out that until the 1200's, people rejected the idea of witchcraft. Of course they believed in such things as poisoning by magic, or the creation of thunder and lightning by sorcerers. But they did not believe that witches could ride through the air or did business with the Devil.

Ireland, however, was different. In the 800's, the church stated that a belief in broomstick riding and vampirism went against the teachings of Christianity. And people who still confessed to this belief were given heavy penance.

Then came the Middle Ages, a time of plague, famine, and political and religious disorders. It seemed that the religious leaders began to equate a disbelief in the teachings of the church with witchcraft. Anyone who did not

A picture of a witch,
drawn about 1537.
This is a copy of a woodcut
made by the famous artist, Holbein.

believe in the established religion must, therefore, believe in the teachings of the Devil. And the Book of Exodus says, "Thou shalt not suffer a witch to live."

The witch mania really began toward the end of the 1400's. Judges were appointed to conduct investigations and hold trials for anyone accused of being a witch. It would seem, from reading the records of these trials that there were more witches on the Continent of Europe than there were in England—or at least there were more who confessed to being witches. But this can be explained by observing that torture was a common thing in Continental Europe, while in England only the highest courts could inflict torture. So, European "witches" confessed in order to be put to death quickly, and save themselves from being tortured to death, while English "witches" died without confessing. But witches were executed anyway, and the English ones were just as dead as if they had confessed.

It would seem that these judges were extremely cruel. But actually, they thought of themselves as good men. Were they not working for the glory of God and the supression of evil? One of them, Nicolas Remy, sentenced nearly nine hundred French people to be burned at the stake in the fifteen years from 1575 to 1590. Toward the end of his life he began to get guilt feelings. These came, not from the deaths he had caused, but rather because he had not executed a few children. He felt it was not right to "spare baby vipers." Probably the champion judge was Peter Binsfeld, Bishop of Treres, who sentenced some six thousand, five hundred people to death by burning.

The judges who conducted witchcraft trials sometimes traveled from district to district, sending out a directive as they entered each area that all people should look around at their neighbors. And, if these neighbors might possibly be witches, they were to be reported. As a matter of fact, if the townspeople did not report witches, they themselves could be punished. Besides, it was their duty as religious citizens to inform the authorities.

The names of the informers were usually kept a secret. So, the accused (who might have been named as a witch by someone who merely had a grudge against her) was often unaware of the charges or the evidence against her. The people on trial were also considered to be guilty until they could prove themselves to be innocent. But how could they defend themselves when they didn't even know what they were supposed to be guilty of?

Then came the trial. Sometimes, it was said the judge might promise the accused that he would be lenient if the accused would only confess. This sometimes worked. The confession would be given which stated that the accused was really a witch. Then would come the burning. What about the promise of leniency? Well, no one had to keep a promise made to a witch.

When torture was used it was almost always effective. The accused would usually confess. Even when he or she knew that a confession would result in execution, swift death was preferable to more torture. The worst part was that the judges of the trials used the enormous number of confessions as proof that there were huge numbers of witches running around. And this reasoning, in turn, led to more and more trials of more and more witches.

Most of the people accused of being witches (and this is still true in the present day) were women. Until quite recently, women were considered to be mentally and physically weaker than men. They were not given equal educational opportunities. And they were taught to rely on their emotions more than on their reason. Because of this, both the government and the church (which were both controlled by men, of course) felt that women were more easily tempted by the Devil than were men. Some people felt that the Devil, being a man, would naturally prefer female assistants. Add to these feelings the fact that women were less able to defend themselves in court, since they had few legal (and economic) rights, and women seem to have been born losers in the witch hunt. Because of all these things, from now on we will refer to witches as women, although quite a few of them were men.

There were a few heroes who fought this horrible system. One of the first to speak out against the witch hunt was John Weyer (born in Holland and originally called Jan Wier), the physician to Duke William of Cleves. He agreed that women were inferior, and in 1563 he published a book, *De praestigis daemonum et incantationitis ac veneficiis.* It declared witchcraft to be merely a delusion caused by demons who took advantage of the weakness and gullibility of women. This assertion was not very flattering, but at least he believed that witchcraft was not the result of a pact with the Devil. After all, it was thought at that time that demons caused many types of diseases. Thanks to Weyer and those who followed, we now often consider "witches" to be mental cases and treat them as such.

In 1584, Reginald Scot, an Englishman, took an even more modern view of the problem. He said that the whole witch hunt was a combination of "ignorance, illusion, roguery, and false accusation."

A German priest, Father Spee, spent two years as a sort of prison chaplain. He tried to provide as many people as he could with spiritual comfort, and often brought messages from friends and family to those in prison. During the time he spent with those individuals convicted as witches, he accompanied almost two hundred people to the stake. Furthermore, Father Spee was not absolutely sure that the trials were fair or that the reasons for them were even justified. He later wrote a book that accused the judges of the witch trials of inhuman cruelty, and stated that he was convinced that all those people who went to their deaths accused of witchcraft were innocent.

The whole thing began to die out in Europe in the early 1500's, and in England in the early 1700's. But it did not die out completely. Even the late outbursts in New England in 1691 and 1692 were not the last gasp of the witch hunt. In Spain the Inquisition was burning witches as late as 1781, and in Germany as late as 1793. In Peru, a woman was burned at the stake in 1888.

It may be true that we no longer burn accused witches at the stake, but there are many self-confessed witches among us today. In the light of modern-day common sense, therefore, let's take a look at who and what they were. Now, how do we define a witch?

The first thing that must be done if a witch is to be defined is to throw out a lot of words. Books have been written that contain more than a thousand pages and still do not include all the varieties of witches. So let's eliminate some terms.

The first two words to ignore are *wizard* and *warlock.* These are really fancy terms for types of male witches. But a witch, male or female, is a witch.

Then there is the word *magician.* This word, which used to be a fine term to describe a person who was able to perform supernatural acts, has come to mean someone, perfectly human, who fools and confuses a theatre audience from a stage. The term doesn't seem to have punch any more, so out it goes.

For the purpose of this book, we have to eliminate *medicine man, shaman, witch doctor,* and all the rest of those dealers in the supernatural who are found mainly in Africa and Asia and in various Indian tribes. This book is too short to include any other type of witch than those involved with the idea of worshiping the concept of the Devil. We can only consider, then, the witches who are found within the Christian culture of the Western World.

For the time being, we will also have to eliminate the practitioner of *White Magic.* There are, of course, many white witches in the Western World. There are witches who cure diseases in Sicily, some who remove spells from farms in France, and many more. But these witches seem to be a modern offshoot of the mainstream of witchery, since they appear rarely in historical records.

Finally, let's eliminate the *sorceress* and *sorcerer.* These are the persons (sometimes called black magicians) who can do many things that witches can do. They can cast spells, charms, and hexes; they can make a love potion or stir up a type of awful concoction as did Macbeth's friends; they can make demons appear, and may even sell their souls to the Devil. But they are selfish. They are doing all of this to gain something for personal reasons, perhaps money or power, fame or pleasure—in this world.

Not so the witch. Reportedly, she can do all of the things that a sorcerer can do, and perhaps more, but she does them for a different reason. It's been acknowledged that everything she does, she does to serve the Devil. She worships him, and therefore hates God. In short, she is a messenger from Hell.

So, every witch is a sorcerer, but not every sorcerer is a witch. Now let's get on with the story.

TWO / JOINING THE GROUP / Suppose a person wanted to become a witch. There have always been ceremonies of admission to witches' organizations. They may have been simple initiations or complex pageants, but most of them had two essential parts. The first requirement is that the candidate is suppose to join of her own free will and accord. The second is that she should devote herself, body and soul, to the Devil.

If we really want to understand witchcraft, we must first face up to the fact that, to the witch, the Devil is God. He may take many forms, but he is the object of worship. Although the men and women who persecuted witches looked upon the Devil (sometimes calling him Satan, Lucifer, the Foul Fiend, Beelzebub, the Enemy of Salvation, etc.) as the Prince of Evil, the witches knelt to him, prayed to him, offered thanks to him, and even dedicated their children to him.

So when a witch would refer to her God, or her Lord, she was speaking of the Devil. But when non-witches talked of this person, they were translating the word "God" into "the Devil."

There are records of witches being visited by the Devil. At least, that is what they said happened. In these cases, they would sometimes describe him as a strange-looking creature having cloven feet, riding a black horse, and so on. But most often he took the form of a man or, on occasion, a woman. At the large meetings of witches, he was disguised in weird costumes. At the small meetings, or when he was visiting a single witch, or when he was trying to tempt someone into witchhood, he would appear as an ordinary man, identifying himself with a certain sign, or a particular article of clothing, such as a specially designed shoe.

The Devil often had an assistant. In the cases where the Devil took the form of a man, this junior fiend was usually a younger man. But when the Devil took the form of a woman, an older man was usually her assistant. Let us admit to ourselves right now, however, that it is quite possible that these "devils" might have been ordinary men, out to gain a little glory and make a little money.

There have been cases in which the Devil was reported to have appeared as a man well-dressed, dressed in tatters, dressed in a multi-colored coat, and dressed in black.

A group of witches presenting a child to the Devil. Perhaps the youngster will become a human sacrifice, or be dedicated to the company of witches.

Devils and demons
were not often very pretty.
Here is a picture of one,
dating from 1555,
showing a creature with a human head
and a dragon's body.

Sometimes he was young, sometimes old. Sometimes he was handsome, sometimes he was ugly. Sometimes he called himself the Devil, sometimes he had a grander title. Sometimes he called himself by common names, such as Daniel, and, in one case, by the simple name of Thom Reid.

When he appeared as an ugly man, he must have really been ugly. In one instance, he was described as being clad in a black gown with a black hat upon his head. His face was terrible, his nose was like the beak of an eagle. He had great, burning eyes. His hands and legs were very hairy, with claws upon his hands. All of this and cloven feet, too.

Then there were times when the Devil appeared as an animal. He usually took the form of a bull, cat, dog, goat, horse, or sheep. The goat or sheep form, strangely enough, seemed to occur only in France. Another unusual fact is that he was never reported to take on the form of a rabbit, although this is a very common animal for a witch to change into. He also is never described in the form of a toad, even though the toad is supposed to be an evil animal often used by witches in connection with their magic. He never seems to have appeared as a fox, a donkey, or a pig, either, although these beasts were, and still are, quite common animals in the Western World.

Of course, witches could never admit that the Devil in animal form was really a man in animal disguise, even when the Devil appeared wearing no costume except an animal mask.

But back to the initiations. They might differ depending on whether the candidate was a child or an adult. For example, in the case of a young French girl in the late 1500's who claimed that she was introduced to the Devil by her boyfriend, it was only necessary to make the sign of the cross with her left hand. This seemed to be enough to get her into the club. But even very small children usually went through a much more complicated ceremony.

The typical initiation might start when the witch-to-be is introduced to the Devil who, usually in human form, is believed to be the one in charge of the meeting. The introduction is made by another witch. This is like the presentation of a baby to a clergyman by the godparents at a Christian baptism. And it probably was a way of vouching for the sincerity of the initiate—a pretty smart move during the days of the witch hunt. After all, the initiate might be an informer and so should be properly investigated.

Then may follow a spoken denial of the Christian faith. In this section, such statements are made as: "I deny my baptism;" "I forsake God and Christ;" or "I believe in the Devil and adhere to him."

Having given up her Christian baptism, the future witch may be rebaptized—this time in the Devil's name. At this

In this picture from the Compendium Maleficarum, *drawn by Guazzo, we see the Devil wiping out the future witch's baptismal markings with his claw.*

time the novice may be renamed, since her original title was a "Christian" name.

Perhaps the Devil will then symbolically remove the Christian baptismal markings by touching the initiate on the forehead. Then the former godparents are denied and new sponsors are appointed from the group of witches in the audience.

Next, a gift of clothing may be given to the Devil as a sign of submission to his demands. An oath of allegiance

is now given by the witch-to-be, while she is standing in a magic circle.

As the ceremony draws to a close, the name of the new witch is written in the "Book of Death." She then may promise to sacrifice children to the Devil and to pay yearly tribute in the form of black-colored gifts, or to destroy holy Christian relics and to keep the secrets of the witches. At the end, the Devil marks her with the "Devil's Mark," and she is officially a member in good standing of the witches sorority.

The woodcut on the left shows the initiate giving a Bible to the Devil as a gift, while the Devil gives him a copy of the Black Book. Finally, the witches-to-be trample on the cross.

This "Devil's Mark" was thought to be a sure sign that the accused was a witch. Most of the time, however, the "Mark" was really a natural birthmark, a scar, a freckle, a wart, a mole, or even a dimple on the chin.

There were times when the witch was asked to sign an agreement, or covenant, to do the Devil's bidding. She usually wrote her signature in blood. These covenants were most often valid for the rest of the witch's life, but sometimes the witch signed up for only a few years—seven being the usual number.

Here is an example of one of these covenants. It was an agreement between the Devil and a renegade French priest, Louis Gaufridi.

> *I, Louis, a priest, renounce each and every one of the spiritual and corporal gifts which may accrue to me from God, from the Virgin, and from all the saints, and especially from my patron John the Baptist, and the Apostles Peter and Paul and St. Francis. And to you, Lucifer, now before me, I give myself and all the good I may accomplish, except the returns from the sacrament in the cases where I may administer it; all of which I sign and attest.*

Then the Devil makes his promise.

> *I, Lucifer, bind myself to give you, Louis Gaufridi, priest, the faculty and power of bewitching by blowing with the mouth, all and any of the women and girls you may desire; In proof of which I sign myself Lucifer.*

This agreement might not hold up in a court of law, but Gaufridi probably thought twice about breaking the covenant. It was surprising how much power the mere mention of the Devil's name had with people.

But suppose that a person did not really want to become a witch. There were ways for the Devil to overcome this reluctance, and one of the most common involved two types of supernatural creatures: the incubus and the succubus.

An incubus is a spirit or demon in male human form, sent by the Devil to seduce prospective female witches. A succubus is a similar creature in female form who seduces prospective male witches.

It was believed that the duty of these demons was to lead innocent humans into sexual sin. This was not mere human sexual sin, since the incubus and succubus were not really human. It was because of this double sin—human and supernatural—that it seemed logical for the seduced person to give up his normal way of life and join the witches. It was probably felt that such a monstrous misdeed could never be forgiven by the church authorities.

There have been stories that sometimes an incubus and a succubus might have offspring from each other, without having had human partners. These "children" were called *cambions,* and supposedly they showed no signs of life until they had reached the age of seven. One story tells of a man on horseback who rode up to a little child (supposedly a cambion) who was trying to cross a stream. The horseman picked up the child and started across the stream. But the cambion was so heavy that the poor horse sank from sight and drowned.

If all else, including promises of riches or help in gaining revenge on enemies, failed, it was said that the Devil could still recruit a witch by demonic possession. He could send a demon to gain control of a human by force. This demon

Sometimes demons were said
to shower their victims with riches,
but when the time came
to claim the poor unfortunate's soul. . . .

would actually take over the body and mind of the poor unfortunate. This was done by entering the body of the victim, but without interfering with the soul of the recruit.

It is a little hard to pin down the thousands of historical reports about demonic possession. To begin with, the rest of the people in a town were apt to be a bit sympathetic about the whole thing. After all, when the victim acted and spoke as one possessed, it was really the demon inside her that was causing all the trouble. So the poor thing could not really be held responsible.

On the other hand, there was a certain amount of feeling that a truly good person could not be possessed. But the good person could be obsessed. That is, the demons, not being able to enter the body, could work on the victim from the outside. It was obsession, not possession, that was supposedly tried on St. Anthony. In his case, time and time again, a demon assumed the shape of a woman and tempted Anthony to sin. This did not work, so finally

Many saints were said to have been tempted by demons. This picture by Michael Pacher, shows St. Wolfgang being approached by the Devil.

Anthony was approached by a huge demon who offered his services. St. Anthony, however, merely spat in his face.

Another reported example of obsession is the case of the Abbé Adam, a French priest who lived in the fourteenth century.

He was traveling along the road when a demon in the form of a white tree rose up in front of him and rushed toward him. The Abbé made the sign of the cross, and the tree disappeared. Then the demon returned again in a different shape. This time he appeared in the form of a black knight, but the Abbé was able to resist still another time.

Again the demon came back, this time in the form of a tall man with a terribly long neck. The Abbé hit him with his fist, and the demon immediately took on the shape of a tiny man wearing a cloak and holding a sword. Again the Abbé made the sign of the cross. Again the demon disappeared, only to return in the shape of first a pig, and then a donkey.

St. Eligius is taking care of a demon who came to obsess him. Eligius was a bishop in the 7th century and the patron saint of all metalworkers. That is probably why he is attacking the demon with the tools of his trade.

This time the Abbé drew a circle in the dirt with a cross inside the circle, all the time shouting at the demon. The demon turned himself into a barrel and rolled into a nearby field, where he then changed himself into a cartwheel. In this form, he was able to roll over the body of the Abbé, but was not able to kill him.

Talk about early morning exercise!

So in either case, obsession or possession, an unwilling person might have been made to behave as a witch. A slightly sinful woman could be possessed. A truly pure woman could be obsessed. And there was another wrinkle. Even the purest woman could be possessed by witchcraft. A witch could cast a spell on her permitting the demon to enter her body and thus to take over.

Now let's stick to possession. When a woman was possessed, here is what was said to have happened. Her face and body would contort, twist, and assume all kinds of strange attitudes. The face would then take on a devilish

ST. ELIGIVS

look and the voice would change. There have been cases of young girls speaking with men's voices. Then, with this new voice, the victim would begin to use foul, blasphemous language, curse God, speak in strange, unknown languages, or just speak gibberish.

Sometimes she lapsed into a quiet state and began to foam at the mouth. Some possessed people, it is reported, vomited needles, pins, broken glass and pottery, hair, bark, and stones. Even harder to believe, were feats requiring enormous strength or rising straight up into the air.

A rather formal list of the symptoms of possession is listed in Spence's *An Encyclopaedia of Occultism.* They are:

1. Imagining oneself possessed.
2. Leading an evil life.
3. Living alone.
4. Chronic ailments, unusual symptoms, a deep sleep, the vomiting of strange things.
5. Blaspheming and frequent reference to the Devil.
6. Making a compact with the Devil.
7. Being controlled by spirits.
8. Having a face that inspires horror and fear.
9. Being tired of living and the giving up of hope.
10. Being enraged and violent in action.
11. Making the cries and noises of a beast.

We can discount much of this. If we are gazing upon someone who is twisting and squirming, speaking a strange language in a strange voice, and foaming at the mouth, we might also be convinced that she is rising into the air and vomiting needles. In a case such as this, it is easy to be inaccurate in our observations. But the rest can be believed. Whether they occur because of possession, certain diseases, or merely because of hysteria, cases of contorted, ranting, cursing people have too often been described by scientists for us to disbelieve them.

As was said before, cases of possession are hard to pin down. We cannot prove that there is no such thing as real possession by a demon. They may also be just examples of hysteria on the part of the local citizens. And in the days of the witch hunts there was a lot to be hysterical about. But there is a third possibility. If the rest of the people were sympathetic toward the person possessed, wouldn't possession serve as an excellent excuse to explain away our sins when we get caught? "It really wasn't my fault. I was possessed by a demon."

So there were probably hundreds of cases of possession reported that had nothing to do with witchcraft.

Now let's imagine a demon gets into a victim, however, how do we get it out? Some churches prescribe definite things for their ministers and priests to do when coaxing out, or exorcising, a demon. This may take the form of a talk between the priest and the demon (who is speaking through the victim). The demon will lie and blaspheme and try in every way to make the priest give up the exorcism. The priest recites prayers, argues with the demon, sprinkles the possessed one with holy water, and holds a crucifix on her.

And if the exorcism proceedings do not seem to be getting anywhere, a process called fumigation may be used. The priest draws a picture of the demon who is possessing the victim, makes the sign of the cross over it, applies holy water, and throws it into the fire. Sometimes the exorcism ceremony goes on for months.

If this seems strange, it should be pointed out that the exorcism ceremony is not too different from the way some psychiatrists treat some of their mentally disturbed patients—particularly those suffering from schizophrenia. Take away the religious symbols and we find that the doctor is also debating in the same way as the priest—but with the unfortunate half of a split personality rather than with a demon.

The rite of exorcism is not too common today. Indeed, the last mention of it in the history of the Anglican Church occurred during the time of Edward VI, when the liturgy contained these directions:

Then let the priest, looking upon the children at the time of their baptism, say, "I command thee, unclean spirit, in the name of the Father, of the Son, and of the Holy Ghost, that thou come out and depart from these infants, whom our Lord Jesus Christ has vouchsafed to call to His holy baptism, to be made members of His Body and of His Holy congregation. Therefore, thou cursed spirit, remember thy sentence, remember thy judgement, remember the day to be at hand wherein thou shalt burn in fire everlasting prepared for thee and thy angels. And presume not hereafter to exercise any tyranny towards these infants whom Christ hath bought with His precious blood, and by His holy baptism calleth to be of his flock."

But this service was dropped shortly after 1550.

The rite of exorcism does exist in the Eastern Orthodox Church today, where it is believed possible that demons might have an influence over mental diseases. In the Roman Catholic Church, it is also possible to carry out the rite, but the parish priest must get permission from his bishop to do it. In most cases, the only time we hear of exorcism going on is in a baptism. Then the person to be baptized (or his godparents, in his name) renounces the Devil.

At the time of the Protestant Reformation, the followers of Martin Luther included exorcism in the practices of the church, but Lutherans soon gave them up. Although the Church of Sweden does not practice exorcism, the Swedish Lutheran Church in the United States, in the 1800's, brought it back when it merged with other churches to form the Lutheran Church in America. Calvinist churches, such as the Presbyterians and the Congregationalists (now a part of the United Church of Christ) have always rejected exorcism because they could find no justification for it in the Bible.

There are other, more crude, and essentially non-religious methods of exorcism practiced in the world, even today. Sometimes the townspeople will throw stones after the possessed woman. This is supposed to frighten the demon out of her. Sometimes they will beat her with strips of leather to force the demon out of her. And, since it is believed that the best way for a witch to cause a demon to enter a person's body is to put a curse on a bit of food and feed it to the victim, sometimes exorcisms take the form of trying to force the bewitched woman to vomit in order to get rid of the enchanted food.

Witches, as you have just read, are created in many ways, through design or by accident, willingly or unwillingly. And whether the individual is possessed or obsessed, it is really only the beginning. There are many questions that have yet to be answered. What happens next?

THREE / CEREMONIES AND FEASTS / In the early days of witchcraft, the witch was looked upon as just a worker of magic. But when the witch hunts of the late Middle Ages began, the idea of the witch as a Devil-worshipper became more popular. And so, the festivals, rites, and ceremonies of witchcraft took on a new importance. The most popular form of assembly, at least the most talked-about, was the Witches Sabbath.

This ceremony is often called the *Sabbat*, and there is a great deal of argument about where the name came from. There are some who say that the term was taken from the name of the ancient Thracian god, Sabazius, who was also worshipped in ceremonies involving a lot of frantic activity. Others say that the name is derived from the French *s'esbettre*, which means to frolic.

The most popular theory is that it came from the Hebrew word sabbat, which is the term for the seventh day, the day of rest in the Old Testament. This seems very likely, since the days of the witch hunts were also days of terrible anti-semitism—hatred of the Jews. Indeed, the Witches Sabbath was sometimes called the *synagoga*, or synagogue. Perhaps these terms were picked up because people connected witches and Jews—or, more likely, just because anything to do with Jews seemed mysterious and sinister to the Christians of that time. Or perhaps the term sabbat was merely a form of the Christian Sabbath: many other elements of witchcraft were inverted or adapted versions of Christian ritual, and the name might come from the same source.

Although Sabbat is Saturday to Jews, and Sabbath is Sunday to Christians, the witches were not so particular. They could hold this gathering on any night of the week, although Thursdays and Fridays seemed to be their favorites, at least for local meetings.

These local meetings for small groups of witches could be held every week, like lodge meetings, but they were not nearly as exciting as the large Sabbats, which included many local groups. Let's skip the small groups, for the time being, and get on to the big conventions. Their dates might have varied slightly from country to country, but the British festivals can serve as examples.

The large Sabbats were usually held six times a year. There were four seasonal meetings and two witches' holiday meetings. They usually began about midnight and lasted until the first cock crowed at dawn.

The first seasonal Sabbat of the year was held on February 2—that is, beginning at the midnight that ended the day of February 1. This is the winter festival of Candlemas in the Christian calendar. The second seasonal Sabbat was the spring festival, held on June 23, the Eve of St. John the Baptist.

Next came August 1. This is the summer festival of the Gule of August, which is called Lammas Day in England. Finally there was the autumn festival of St. Thomas, on December 21. In the seventeenth century, in Scotland, the spring festival was switched to May 3 (Holy Cross) and the autumn festival was rescheduled on November 1 (All Saints' Day).

The two biggest nights of the year, however, were April 30 and October 31. April 30 is the Eve of May Day—the Grand Sabbat—called Roodmas or Rood Day in England, and in Germany called *Walpurgisnacht* (Walpurgis Night), named after St. Walburga, whose commemorative day is the first of May. Walburga was an English nun who joined a mission to Germany. In 761 she became the head of the monastery at Heidenheim, where she died in either 777 or 779—no one knows for sure. The fact that Walpurgis night was the same night when the ancient druids made their annual sacrifices caused her to become associated in people's minds with witchcraft.

October 31 is the date of All Hallows' Eve, which is the day when even little children dress up as witches—Hal-

Bruegel inuent

A Sabbat.
In this picture
by Breughel the Elder,
from the 1500's,
we see St. James
trying to stop
the festivities.

lowe'en. All Hallows' Eve is supposed to be the night when the Devil and his witches hold their greatest power. It is also, according to superstition, one of the best nights of the year to predict the future. For example, on this night, one can predict who will be his or her future marriage partner.

Get an apple and on the stroke of midnight go alone into a room containing a mirror. Cut the apple into small pieces and throw one of the pieces over your left shoulder. Don't look back, but eat the other pieces while combing your hair and looking into the mirror. While you are doing this, the face of your future husband or wife will appear in the mirror, looking over your left shoulder.

Or you can eat a piece of salt herring on All Hallows' Eve. In your dreams, your future husband or wife will appear to offer you a drink of water to quench your terrible thirst.

You can also, on Hallowe'en, find out whether or not your marriage will be happy. Take two nuts and place them in a fire. Name one of them after yourself and the other after your future marriage partner. If they burn side by side, the marriage will be happy. But if they move apart, the marriage will not be successful.

Now let's get along to the big Sabbat. Once the great day arrived, the witches had to use their witchcraft just to get to the meeting. Only a few lived close enough to walk.

Some, of course, were able to get there on horseback. But the rest of them had to find other means of transportation.

They had to fly, and there were three ways of doing this. They could fly unsupported (presumably carried by an invisible demon), they could be supported by a stick, or they could be riding on a flying animal, usually a horse. But before they could fly, they had to rub a magic ointment on their bodies.

Here is a recipe for one of those magical ointments:

1. Take the fat from the bodies of young children.
2. Boil the fat in water in a brass pot.
3. Take the thick part of the mixture and add "eleosolinum, aconitum, frondes populeas," and soot.
4. Then add "sium, acarum vulgare, pentaphyllon," the blood of a bat, "solanum somniferum, and oleum."
5. Stamp all these together and smear the resulting ointment on the body.

This ointment may not have been sufficient to get the job done. In case the stuff didn't work, the witch was advised to use magic words to get her off the ground. On the way to the meeting, she was supposed to say, "Thout, tout a tout, tout, throughout and about." And on the way home, "Rentum, Tormentum."

When it came to riding on a stick or broom, or a flying animal, there were usually two main methods. If the object

Off to the Sabbat. One witch is flying out of the chimney, three others are preparing to take off, and a curious boy is spying on them.

were really a demon in disguise, the witch could jump on and fly away. Some witches had magic bridles that could transform an ordinary stick into something that could fly.

Before they could be off, however, witches sometimes had to protect themselves. If they were married to non-witches, it would be hard to explain their ability to fly off into the night to their husbands. So, obviously, witches had to put a spell on those people who might observe their method of transportation. This was most often done by putting them to sleep for a time.

The Sabbat was usually held on one of several fixed sites. Some reports have suggested that it was held near a lake, stream, or pond—anyway, near water of some kind. And the place often contained a standing stone. Other reports tell of witches meeting on top of a mountain or in a forest clearing. In any case, usually the idea was to stay as far away from human habitation as possible.

Some of the most popular places were the Brocken Peak in Germany, the top of the Puy-de-Dôme in France, and the Blocula, a meadow in Sweden. In the United States, there was to have been a meeting place in a grassy field, near Salem, Massachusetts.

There were no definite number of witches that were required to hold a Sabbat. It was considered convenient if there were an equal number of male and female witches there, but if one sex or the other was outnumbered, things could be evened up by having the proper number of incubi or succubi on hand. Sometimes a non-witch, if she had special connections, could attend.

Some Sabbats had fewer than ten witches in attendance. But one held near Ferrara, Italy, according to a sixteenth-century witch's confession, had six thousand present, and in the seventeenth century near Valpute, France, ten thousand showed up.

But now the festivities are about to begin. Let's look at a possible Sabbat in continental Europe. All of the witches have gathered, and they stand there, with their naked bodies still shining from their magic ointments, some holding burning black candles. The Devil, or one of his demons, presides. He may be seen in the form of a black goat or ram. When the Devil appeared in the shape of a he-goat, he was often referred to by the name of *Bachelor* or *Baphomet.* One description of this form is a goat head, human hands, a belly covered with scales, and feathers covering the rest of the body, except for the chest, where there were female breasts.

The Devil may also be seen as a figure with horns, bat wings, and hooves. Or he may be seen in human form, wearing a horned mask and headdress. He may be seated upon his black throne or standing on an altar. Now the witches begin to gather around.

The first order of business is for the witches to pay homage to the Devil. First they must renew their vows of obedience. They may present him with gifts, such as black candles. Then they must kiss him on any part of his anatomy that he directs them to—but most often on his buttocks. This act is called the *osculum infame* or kiss of shame. Much bowing and scraping follows this.

A litany is now sung. These litanies took many forms, but one of the catchiest is this one:

Lucifer, Beelzebub, Leviathan, have pity on us.

Baal, prince of the seraphim; Baalberith, prince of the cherubim; Astaroth, prince of the thrones; Rosier, prince of denominations; Carreau, prince of the powers; Belial, prince of the vertues; Perrier, prince of the principalities; Oliver, prince of the archangels; Sarceuil, Fume-bouche, Pierre-le-Feu, Carviveau, Terrier, Contellier, Candelier, Behemoth, Oilette, Belphegor, Sabathan, Garandier, Dolers, Pierre-Fort, Axaphat, Prisier, Kakos, Lucesme, pray for us.

You may notice the similarity of form to the *kyrie eleison* used in some Christian churches.

Next comes the old business. Here come the reports of all of the magic done since the last meeting, either by individuals or groups of witches. And at the same time, the witches may consult with the Devil to gain hints on how to carry out their current plans for witchery.

Then comes the new business. There may be some witch initiates to be confirmed. There may even be witch couples who want to be married by the Devil. This part of the Sabbat is concluded by the sacrifice of an animal—perhaps a goat, a dog, a cat, or a chicken. And following all this come the real festivities.

The banquet could be eaten either outdoors or indoors, depending on the weather or the country. In southern France the banquet was almost always an outdoor picnic. In Scotland and Sweden, it was almost always held indoors. In England, it all depended on the temperature or the rainfall. Usually, outdoors or indoors, huge tables were spread, but there are cases where the outdoor picnic was laid out on blankets on the ground.

Sometimes the Devil supplied the food, and sometimes one of the members of the witch community would foot the bill. There were cases where every witch brought her own picnic basket. But no matter where the food came from, the participants would say a little type of grace to the Devil. They thought that it was from him that all the food came.

Was the food good? In some cases it seemed that it really was foul and disgusting, and that no matter how much the witches ate, their appetites were not satisfied. Reports of this kind usually came from young girls who may not have had highly developed taste buds. Or it may be that they were so worn out from the wild dancing that followed the feast that they were soon hungry again.

Most reports, however, were of truly sumptuous feasts. There were wines and liquors, huge platters of meat (some say meat from the babies stolen by witches), and many other dainties. In some countries no salt was used since this chemical is supposed to be a hex against witches. As we would expect, table manners were not too important, the witches seldom using knives or forks.

Once the banquet is over, on with the dance. At times the witches merely danced simple country dances. But more often the dances were used for magical purposes. There were jumping dances that were supposed to make the crops grow high. There were fertility dances that were supposed to increase the birth rate, and, if the witches dressed up like animals, this would increase the number of domestic animals to be born.

These magic dances were usually of two types. The first type was a ring dance, sometimes conducted around a stone, a maypole, or even around the Devil himself. In this one, the witches danced back to back.

And the second dance resembled a game of follow the leader. But whatever dances they did, they did them riotously and rapidly. They certainly were excited, whether from the wild musical accompaniment, the wine they had had at the banquet, or (as sometimes happened) that they were dancing without clothes.

Besides all of this, it was recorded there were times when the witch who couldn't keep up with the rest was severely punished. This was especially true in the follow-the-leader dance. The Devil was said to beat on the witch at the end of the line if she couldn't stay with the group—probably the origin of the phrase "the Devil take the hindmost."

The music for the dance could be both vocal and instrumental. Oftentimes the Devil himself would be the musician, but others could take his place. The soloist would play the pipes of Pan, a Jew's harp, or some other simple mouth instrument. Sometimes a tambourine was used. When singing was a part of the music, the songs were usually quite filthy, and all of them were sung in praise of the Devil.

Toward the end of the Sabbat came a wild orgy, usually begun by the Devil, and eventually including all of the members present. Then came the crowing of the first rooster at dawn, and the witches, exhausted, would wend their weary ways home.

Some experts in the field of the study of witchcraft refer to another type of meeting—the *Esbat.* This was a business meeting, in contrast to the Sabbat, which was more of a religious festival. While both of these meetings ended with feasting and dancing, the Esbat was called for the purpose of practicing magic. Here was where the whole group of witches would work on a few problems—helping a human client harm his enemy, for example.

Sometimes Esbats were called in order to open graves to steal the bones of dead men, women, and children. These could then be used as magical charms. Sometimes Esbats were called for blasphemous purposes, such as the christening of a cat or other animal. Sometimes they were called for the purpose of planning a campaign—to wreck a ship, for example, or to get a fellow witch out of prison. Or perhaps they would be called for the purpose of mere deviltry and a little fun, such as to create a thunderstorm and thus ruin a planned outdoors event, maybe a town fair or a summer festival.

These meetings were not as large as the Sabbats. They were usually held on a certain day of the week, but there was no fixed hour. Sometimes, they were even called in the daytime. When an Esbat was being planned, the Devil himself set the day and hour. He then told his followers about it personally or sent a message around with an officer of the group. And then the magic began.

A witch
busy about her work
—this time,
the creation of
a thunderstorm.

FOUR / THE SACRIFICE AND OTHER SPORTS /

At various times it has been noted that witches or groups of witches would be called upon to make sacrifices—all of them pretty grisly. There were four basic kinds; the blood sacrifice, the animal sacrifice, the human sacrifice, and the Devil sacrifice.

The blood sacrifice was the most common, and also the most simple, since it was the witch's own blood that was to be spilled. This was done when a new witch joined the clan. Actually, the sacrifice came to be a part of the signing of the contract at the initiation. This was probably because there was a contract to be signed and, with all that lovely blood flowing, what could be more natural than to use the witch's own blood instead of bothering with ink?

It is said that, at times, the Devil gave the witch-to-be a bone to gouge herself with. And when the blood began to flow he would suck it out of the wound and drink it. There are other cases of the Devil causing the blood to flow from the initiate's mouth or shoulder. There was a case in

1662 where the Devil added an additional section to the initiation and baptized the witch in his own name by sucking out a mouthful of blood, spitting it into his hand, and sprinkling it on her head.

Another popular sport among witches was the sacrifice of animals. It seems that this was so common, however, that many details about the technique were rarely given. It probably was not dramatic enough to talk about. So trifling was it that the sacrifice seldom happened at a witches' meeting, but was usually done by a single witch in the peace and quiet of her own home.

The purpose of killing an animal, usually a dog, a cat, or a chicken, was a personal one. It could be a sort of thank-offering, or perhaps was used as a plea to obtain help from the Devil. There are those who say that witches were required to sacrifice an animal every day, just on general principles. But that is probably an exaggeration. It is an old rite, and the earliest recorded witch trial in the British Isles, held in 1324, involved the sacrifice of animals.

Many stories mention that the Devil would come to the witch and make a request for a certain number of specific types of animals to be sacrificed. Then, when the menu had been decided upon, the sacrifices would be made, and the Devil would eat the animals. It is often said that, after he ate the animals, not a trace of bone, fur, or feathers could be found.

The human sacrifice was quite a bit more complicated. To begin with, it was usually the sacrifice of a child. The object was probably a witch's child or a normal—but unbaptized—baby. In short, the child was one who did not belong to the Christian way of life. This is, by the way, one of the reasons why people of the Middle Ages considered an unbaptized child to be in great danger and why they were in so much of a hurry to rush their newborn offspring off to a priest.

One account gives a horrible picture of the technique of child sacrifice. The child, snatched from its mother's side during the night, was held up into the air and a needle was thrust through its brains. Then the child was burned. There have been shortcuts mentioned, also, such as the burning of a child who had died recently. And perhaps the little one might have been killed by poisoning.

These children were said to have been killed as a sacrifice to the Devil, but sometimes a child had to be killed for another reason. This was done as a means of getting valuable materials for the purpose of making witch's brews, as was mentioned in connection with the magic flying ointments. Accounts have been written of witches boiling children. The thickened parts of their remains were used in ointments, and the thinner parts were set aside to be drunk by the witches to obtain additional magic powers.

Sometimes just the inner organs were distilled and

drunk. Sometimes only the feet, the hands, or a part of the head were eaten (in one case reported as being baked in a pie!). The purpose of this last technique was to seal the lips of the witch that she might never confess her sins. The idea was that if you eat the flesh of a human who has never learned to talk, you will be unable to tell of the horrors that you have committed.

The sacrifice of the Devil is sometimes referred to as the sacrifice of the God, since the Devil was the god of the witches. This had to be done periodically—every one, seven, or nine years, depending on the group of witches—and often an animal, such as a goat, was substituted for the Devil.

But there seem to have been cases in which a human was used as a substitute for the Devil. Believe it or not, some of these human pinchhitters were volunteers. Other substitutes were witches who were bound for public execution for witchcraft anyway.

The substitute, whether it was an animal or a human, was first given the power and rank of the Devil for whom he was to die. For a period of time, he was permitted to live, and, in the case of the human sacrifice, was given special favors usually only given to the Devil. Then the substitute was killed. If it was an animal, it was burned. But if it was a convicted witch, the public executioner would do the job (without knowing that he was assisting the witches).

Very often these sacrificial bodies were then burned and their ashes scattered.

Another thing witches were quite concerned with was fertility. It may well be that originally they busied themselves with both increasing and decreasing the supply of crops, animals, and humans. But by the time of the witch hunt, it was felt they were happiest when they were causing crops to fail and animals to stop reproducing. In fact, the original statement by Pope Innocent VIII, in 1488—the one that started the whole witch hunt, said that witches "blight the marriage bed, destroy the births of women, and prevent the increase of cattle; they blast the corn on the ground, the grapes of the vineyard, the fruits of the trees, and the grass and herbs of the field." That's quite an accusation.

During the reign of Queen Elizabeth I, in England, a cattle disease appeared, causing the cows to go blind. In Ireland, at that time, witches called "eyebiters" were believed to be the cause of the blindness. Many of the women suspected of causing the epidemic were executed.

There is reason to think that witches have always been involved with fertility. The scattering of the ashes of their sacrifices as well as many of their recorded incantations and their preserved charms tell us this.

Sometimes witches desired to cause wide-spread fertility, such as an increase of crops or animals in a whole district. In cases like this, the whole witch group might participate.

At other times, perhaps only the fertility of a particular animal, woman or field was being increased. In this case, only one or two witches were necessary.

One of the best ways to increase the fertility of a farmer's field is to make rain. Witches have reportedly always been able to do this. They can also cause hail to fall upon the fields of a farmer that they are not too fond of. Rain was sometimes made merely by throwing a flint stone over the left shoulder toward the west, or throwing sea sand up into the air. Sometimes a broom would be wetted and the water sprinkled in the air, or a pit would be dug in the ground and filled with water. Boiling hog bristles was sure-fire, as was the burying of the herb, sage, until it became rotten.

How can it be that increasing fertility is the work of the Devil? Actually, this magic was done to help the Devil. Fields were made fertile in order for witches' food to grow there, and sometimes they were made fertile in order for thorns and brambles to grow better—thus playing a pretty nasty joke on the farmer. Animals and women were sometimes made fertile for future animal sacrifices or a child might be born who would eventually become a witch.

Witches often were accused of preventing fertility. Men complained that an accused witch had made them impotent, while women said that witches had made their milk dry up. But whether a witch increased fertility or decreased it, her purpose was to serve her master, the Devil.

Sometimes witches had left-over magic. This witch is trying to sell a storm to a group of sailors, while a male witch has captured the winds and holds them by a rope with three knots in it.

FORNI CATVS. ES
PERIVRVS. ES.
ECCE. PECCATA. TVA
AVARE. VIXISTI
OCCIDISTI

FIVE / WITCH POWER / For hundreds of years, the witch was a convenient thing to have around, at least for one purpose. Almost anything that went wrong, from a death in the family to a mug of milk that went sour, could be blamed on witches' magic. A stillborn infant, a dead cow, a poor crop, a fire in the house, a plague of locusts, a sunken ship — any tragedy, large or small, could be blamed on a witch and her evil doings.

Sometimes a non-witch would use a witch as a consultant. Perhaps there was a love potion to be brewed so that a man could attract a woman. Or perhaps a poisoning was in order. Maybe a look into the future was wanted.

One of the simplest things that witches were said to be able to do involved very little work on their part. There was no mixing of magic potions, or sacrifices. All that needed to be done was to look the victim in the eye. This was the power of the "evil eye," and was used to bewitch someone or even kill him.

◀ *Witches trying to tempt a man on his death-bed.*

Disease could also be caused with a glance, either by the concentrated evil shining out of the witch's eyes or because of evil spirits that flew out of the eyes toward the victim.

There have been stories of the evil eye that told of witches who were able to split mirrors or jewels with a single glance. Others could stare at a bird in the sky and cause it to fall to the ground.

There were many tales of children being enchanted by the evil eye. In order to find out if a child was enchanted or not, one could take three small apples and drop them into a pan of water that had been placed under the baby's cradle. If they floated, the child was not enchanted. If they sank, he was. Or one could cut a piece of bread with a knife that had been marked with three crosses. The bread and the knife were left on the child's pillow all night. If, in the morning, there was rust on the knife, the child was enchanted. And here was a sure test, lick the forehead of a child; if it tasted salty, he was surely enchanted.

There was an English witch of the Middle Ages, Florence Newton, who was able to enchant her victims by kissing them. She supposedly kissed a serving maid who promptly suffered from fits and was mysteriously transported from place to place. Sometimes she ended up on top of a house, sometimes between two feather beds. When Florence was arrested, she kissed her prison guard on the hand, and he promptly dropped dead, so they say.

Another power that witches reportedly had was called *metamorphosis.* This was the ability to turn themselves into animals of all shapes and sizes. Most often the witch would choose a dog, a cat, a rabbit, a toad, or a bird. It was not the purpose of metamorphosis to turn into something horrible. The purpose was to turn into something common, something not particularly noticeable.

If no one noticed the witch, she would be much freer to do her dirty work. Then, too, turning into these animals made it much easier to get into a house, for example. Just fly in through the window as a bird or crawl under the door as an insect. Some believers have said that the power of metamorphosis was given to only a few witches by the Devil. It was a reward for outstanding service.

Sometimes the Devil himself was called upon to work the metamorphosis. This he could do with a single gesture. Most often, however, the witch would cause herself to be metamorphosed. A common method was to utter a magic spell. To turn into a rabbit:

I shall go into a hare
With sorrow and such and care,
And again I shall go in the Devil's name
And will I come home again.

To get back into human form:

Hare, hare
God send thee care.
I am in a hare's likeness just now,
But I shall be in a woman's likeness even now.

All witches were supposed to be able to fly. That is how many of them got to the Sabbat. As was mentioned before, one of the ways of flying was to apply a magic ointment. Recipes for this ointment vary, but almost all of them advise mixing in a little aconite and a little belladonna. Now, aconite will produce excitement when taken internally, and belladonna will cause delirium. And it is possible that if these substances are rubbed hard enough into the skin, they will cause the effect of delirious excitement as if they had been swallowed. Could the trick of flying be just the result of a drugged dream?

But witches also flew on animals, and many people thought that these animals were really demons who had disguised themselves as beasts of burden. They may have been the witches' *familiars.*

Familiars can be divided into two groups, depending on their powers. Some were *divining familiars* and were used to foretell the future. Others were *domestic familiars* and were the servants of the witches.

The divining familiar did not really belong to the witch. It just appeared at the performances of magical ceremonies, and some say that this type of familiar was actually the Devil in disguise. After all, if the Devil is a god, he can predict the future. Not much is known about these strange animals. But it seems that when they appeared, the witch could read her prediction by the direction from which it came, by its speed and actions, and so on. Occasionally, the familiar would turn into the Devil himself and so could speak to the witch and tell her all about the future.

Domestic familiars, sometimes called familiar spirits or familiar imps, were the personal demons of the witches—usually only one to a customer. They sometimes aided the witches in making magic, and they sometimes acted as their servants. No matter what their job was, stories say they strengthened the witch's effectiveness. A familiar was sort of a mother's helper or an extra set of hands.

A witch's familiar could be a dog or a cat, a rabbit or an insect. Some of them were toads. While they were fed ordinary food, the dessert course usually was some of the witch's blood sucked from her body. This blood flowed from a special place on her body called the "witch's mark"; this is not the same thing as the "Devil's mark," which she got at her initiation. The witch usually kept her familiar, since it was such a small animal, in a pot or a box, where it lived on a bed of wool.

Where did the witch get her familiar? The quickest way, it would seem, was as a gift from the Devil himself. These charming presents could be either divining familiars or domestic familiars. They were usually given at the initiation ceremony. But the witch could not keep the present if it were a divining familiar. So it seems that the Devil was merely showing her what kind of animal she should be on the lookout for when she needed to foretell the future. It could be a cat, a dog, or whatever species she would be using in the times to come.

If the gift were a domestic familiar, the witch would be handed the beast along with directions for its care and feeding. Also, its special powers would be explained. It was rare for a witch to be given more than one familiar, but when this happened, it would be pointed out that each had different powers and should be used for a different purpose.

A witch could also be given a familiar by another witch. This was normally a domestic familiar, since only the Devil could create a divining familiar. Sometimes familiars were passed on from mother to daughter. This was a popular method of getting a familiar, since the witch religion has always been hereditary in witch families. But what an awful thing to inherit at the reading of your mother's will!

Finally, a witch could possibly receive a familiar through magical words or actions. One of the most popular ways was to begin at a communion service or a mass at church; this was most effective if it were the person's first communion. When the person received the bread, or host, at the service, she was not to eat it, but rather secretly take it out of her mouth and smuggle it outside the church. Once outside, she would be approached by an animal—a cat, a dog, a toad, or such. She was then to feed the sacramental bread to the animal and accounts say it would then become her domestic familiar.

There have been cases mentioned where a domestic familiar appeared in human form. Female witches would have male familiars and male witches would have female familiars. This probably caused a great deal of talk in the neighborhood, and it is hard to figure out how such a pet could be kept in a pot in the kitchen.

Witches received much of their power through the use of magic words and spells, the example of turning into a rabbit being only one of many. Spells are merely words, written or spoken, that are supposed to have magical effects. And there are several types of spells.

The first kind of spell is used to call up the protection of gods, saints, or even devils. One of the most common of these, but one not used by witches, is:

Matthew, Mark, Luke, and John,
Bless the bed that I lie on.

There were also spells used to gain some small end, such as in mixing a love potion. The most important spell was, of course, the type used to raise the Devil and thereby get his assistance.

One witch, in summoning her divining familiar, yelled, "Elva." When she was through with the dog that appeared, she shouted, "Depart by the law you live on." She was also heard to say, "Hail, hola," when throwing a cat into the sea to cause a storm.

Another witch raised the Devil by saying, "Benedicite," and got rid of him with "Maikpeblis." Another called "Serpent" to the Devil, while another cried "Robin." Swedish witches often shouted: "Antecessor, come and carry us to Blockula."

When starting out to a Sabbat or Esbat, a popular spell was:

Horse and hattock,
Horse and go,
Horse and pellattis, ho! ho!

And when coming back from the meeting:

A boy!
Merry meet,
Merry part.

A cow could be bewitched so that it gave blood instead of milk by saying "Butyrum de armento." In order not to be missed while she was off to a Sabbat, a witch might lay a broom or a stool in her bed, then recite this so that the object took on her form:

I lay down this besom in the Devil's name,
Let it not stir till I come again.

When a witch in animal form paid a social call on another witch, she might enter the house saying, "I conjure thee, go with me." With these words, the second witch would turn into the same kind of animal as her visitor. When they met in the open, the words were, "Devil speed thee, go thou with me," and the same thing would happen.

Then there were the curses. The simplest one was "A pox take it," and the curse would go into effect. A curse a little more complicated was recited over a picture of the person to be cursed: "A pox on thee, I'll spite thee."

A witch was once heard to say, "Drowning by sea and conflagration by land. May you never see a son to follow your body to the graveyard, or a daughter to mourn your death." That's quite a mouthful.

Here is a witch's grace before dinner:

We eat this meat in the Devil's name,
With sorrow, and such, and meikle shame;
We shall destroy house and hall;
Both sheep and goat until the fall.
Little good shall come to the fore.
Of all the rest of the little store.

Actually, none of the spells given here will work. The wording has been slightly changed to protect the innocent.

Obviously, people needed a way to fight against the evil power of witches. Even before the inquisitions there were many ways to get rid of witches. A whip made of elder wood or mountain ash could be used to drive away a witch. Garlic, bay branches, and witch hazel would also turn the trick, and holy water was the best of all. A stone with a hole in it could be strung on a string and worn about the neck to protect an individual; the stone nailed to the door of a house would protect the whole building.

Other ways to protect a house were to hang horseshoes or the metal parts of horses' bridles over the door, or to hang green glass balls in the windows. A very interesting technique was to bury an iron knife under the doorstep. Witches cannot stand iron and this was one of the given reasons why they ate with their hands at their banquets—most tableware contained iron or steel.

If a citizen were afraid of the evil eye, he could make gestures with his hands to ward it off—close the fist and extend the thumb and little finger, thus making the "Devil's Horn." Or close the fist and stick out the index and little finger. Or close the fist and stick the thumb out between the index and middle fingers, which is a symbol of removing the witch's tongue. Or just cross the index and middle fingers, representing the sign of the cross.

A complicated method of avoiding the evil eye is to wear a coat made of material woven on Christmas night in the name of the Devil. Some people even wrote the Lord's Prayer on a piece of paper and carried it in one of their shoes.

There are other remarkable accounts of protections against the evil eye. One can wear, among other things, a piece of hyena's skin taken from its forehead, or the kernel from the fruit of the palm tree. Madwort can be hung up anywhere in the house. We can spit on our right shoe before we put it on, or lick a child's forehead — first up, then across, then up again — and spit behind its back. We can put dirt from a boy's grave under a living boy's pillow, or dirt from a girl's grave under a living girl's pillow. We can drink a glass of water that contains the ashes of a rope that was used to hang a criminal. We can wear bags containing the dust in which a mule has rolled, or lockets containing bones from the right side of a toad's body.

To cancel out a witch's spell, steal a tile from the roof of her house and sprinkle it with a mixture of urine and salt, then heat it. The salt in this mixture is interesting. As was mentioned, many witches did not use salt in their food — it was supposed to be a powerful chemical in the working of white magic.

One of the spells used to drive away the Devil was the word, "Agia." This word is made up of the first letters of the words in an ancient Hebrew saying: "Athah gabor ieolam, Adonai." This means "Thou art powerful and eternal, Lord."

All in all, one of the most popular ways of dealing with witches was a physical one—threaten her life or just beat her up. It was believed, for example, that if a witch were thrown on the ground hard enough to make blood come out of her eyes, all of her spells would be broken. This method must have been almost as hard on the punishers as it was on the witch.

Of course, the witch's house could always be burned down. This was very effective. But the most effective way of all to ward off witches was to lead a virtuous life, since no witch could really harm a religious, righteous, and charitable human being.

SIX / HUNTING WITCHES / Up until the beginning of the 1200's, people did not seem to be too upset about witchcraft. Oh, there were laws against sorcery, conjuring, and divining, but they were not usually enforced. Then came the issue of Devil worship and the idea began to spread that witches were non-Christian. The next thing that happened was the birth of the witch hunt.

Early in the thirteenth century, a persecution was begun in southern France against the Manichaean heretics. These people believed in two gods—one for good and one for evil. They were almost exterminated. Along with the Manichaeans, the Waldensians were persecuted. These people believed in the Bible, but they did not hold with the authority of the Pope.

The persecutions then changed. Heretics—people who reject or oppose the teachings of the established church—began to be accused of witchcraft. Perhaps the first person to be executed for witchcraft during the beginnings of the

Inquisition was a woman accused of having relations with the Devil. She was sentenced to be burned in Toulouse in 1275. In the 1300's, the Inquisition attacked a secret society called the Knights Templar for supposedly worshipping the Devil at their meetings and wrecking holy objects.

But the real beginning of the terror occurred in 1486, when a book, *Malleus Maleficarum* (The Hammer of Witches) was published. This was a handbook for witch hunters. The *Malleus Maleficarum* was written by two German Inquisitors, Jacob Sprenger and Henricus Insistor. It described witchcraft, spelled out the magical practices of witches, and explained Devil worship. It discussed the nature of demons and the ways in which they control human beings. It told why women are more often witches than men, and how witches transform themselves into animals. Guidelines were also given on how to convict witches in the courts. The two authors bragged a bit about themselves, describing how they had been tempted by demons who tried to prevent them from writing the book. They pointed out, however, that they as Inquisitors were too saintly and pure in heart to give in.

The trials of the witches might seem to be extremely unfair. To begin with, the accused was considered guilty until she could prove her innocence. But how could she prove her innocence? It is impossible to prove that something did *not* happen, and there were always a number of witnesses around who would, because of their hysterical fear, swear to anything. Most of the time the accused had no defense attorney. At the time, it was believed that if you defended a witch, you must be a witch yourself. So if the witch had a lawyer, and they lost the case, as usually happened, both the accused and the attorney were liable to be executed.

Then there was the torture used to get the accused to confess. Torture had been approved of by Pope Innocent IV in 1257; this decree was not officially cancelled by the Vatican until 1816.

Often the tortures were not necessary to get a conviction. In the first place, gossip alone was enough to cause a woman to be arrested. Some were arrested whose only crime was to throw water into the air. There seemed always to be someone around who would swear that the poor unfortunate was trying to cause a thunderstorm by means of witchcraft. Sometimes all that the accused had to be was ugly, old, or deformed. On the other hand, if she were attractive and young, she might be called a "bewitching" young lady, and be arrested for witchcraft.

Anyone who had a pet in the house could be a suspect. The pet might be a witch's familiar. So the accused might be put on a chair and tied up in an empty room, and the judges would watch her through a peephole to see if a demon in the shape of an animal would come to see her.

If we think of the filth that existed in medieval jails, it is not hard to imagine that, if the judges waited long enough, a rat or a spider or an insect would sooner or later come into the room. This animal was considered to be a familiar and so obviously the woman was guilty.

Another test to prove that the accused was a witch was to duck her in water. If she were a witch, she would float in the water. The idea behind this little test was that the water was rejecting her, since she herself had rejected the holy water of baptism. Only the innocent sank. But, unfortunately, the innocent one often drowned.

One great way to tell if a woman was a witch or not was called the method of bibliomancy. The suspect was put on one end of a weighing scale and a Bible from the church was put on the other. If the woman weighed less than the Bible, she was innocent. Some church bibles were actually pretty large; in fact, they were often too heavy to carry, and such great weight helped prevent theft.

Sometimes the judges looked for witch's marks or Devil's marks. Almost any kind of spot could be mistaken for the witch's or Devil's mark, and there are very few people without a single mole, birthmark, wart, or scar on their bodies. So the searchers were usually successful and the women were convicted.

Then there was the test called "pricking." Once the mark was found, it was pricked with a pin. If it did not

The "swimming test" of the 1500's. The accused witch is tied in a cloth bag before being thrown into the water.

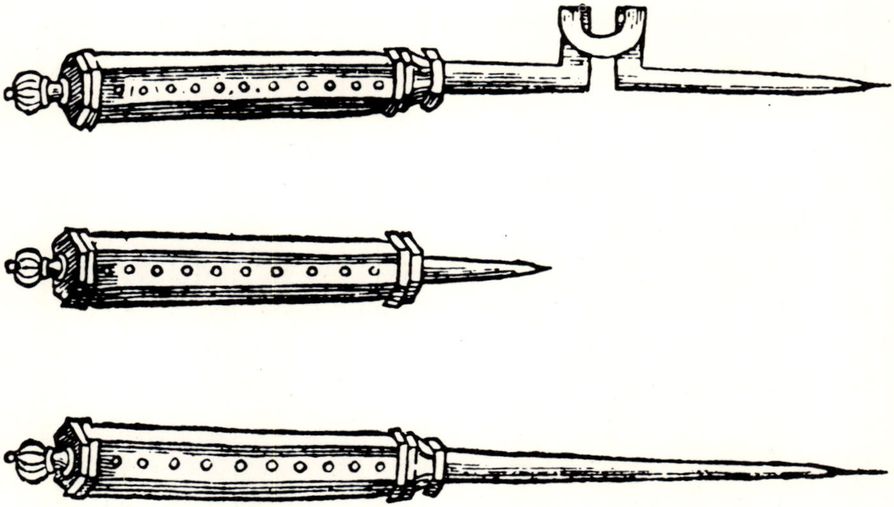

"Prickers" were used to discover "Devil's marks." The two at the bottom have the famous retractable blade, causing neither pain nor bleeding.

hurt or bleed, it was supposed to be truly a mark of a witch and the person was found guilty. Just to make sure, however, the judges thought up the idea of the invisible mark. So they were free to stick pins into the bodies of the accused on almost any point of their anatomy. Many parts of our bodies are almost pain-free—the skin on our heels or an old scar, for example—so it was easy to find an invisible mark. Then, too, it is possible that, having been stripped in public, shaved, and perhaps tortured, the accused might be in such a frame of mind that she would not feel a pinprick. Some Inquisitors have been said to have used fake needles, placed so that when they touched anything, the needle would slide back up into the handle. This would make it rather difficult to feel the prick of the needle, wouldn't it?

It seems that the trials in England were a little more humane than those in Europe; torture was not publicly accepted in Britain. But some judges thought up tortures that would leave no marks on the body, so they might not be said to have been cruel. These judges went in for starvation and the prevention of sleep instead.

The typical sentence for a convicted witch in Europe was burning. In England and in the American colonies later, it was hanging.

Let's imagine a possible witch trial. To begin with, we need a suspect. These are not hard to find, since all that we need is one person willing to accuse another of being a witch. There are many people willing to do this, some of them having a genuine belief in witchcraft. There are others, also, who are merely being spiteful, or are paid by the courts to accuse others, or who are thrill-seekers, or who are just crazy. At certain periods in certain countries, children were encouraged to act as if they were bewitched, then to make ridiculous accusations. So, we will have no trouble in finding an accuser to point out the victim.

Now we hustle the accused off to court. We ask her some questions about her familiars, her worship of the Devil, what she does at Sabbats and Esbats, and the spells that she has worked. At this point she is asked to give the names of other women that she knows to be witches. Perhaps she denies her witchhood, so we look for the marks. Of course, these are found. Now, if she still refuses to confess, we try other means to force her to admit her love for the Devil.

If this trial is taking place in Europe, we might start by whipping the accused. Then we can force her to eat huge quantities of heavily salted meat and refuse to give her water to drink. If we still get no confession, next come the thumbscrews, the leg vises, and the cutting off of fingers. We might put her in the stocks—nasty ones with exposed nails to cut into her flesh, for example. We can stick her with the tips of feathers that have been dipped in sulfur. We can dump her into a mixture of scalding water and lime. We can hoist her off the ground with a rope tied around her wrists and then tie heavy weights to her ankles. We can tickle her with white-hot branding irons. We can put her on a wheel and turn her slowly over a fire.

Most of the accused people eventually confessed. Who wouldn't? Then the witch is hauled back into the courtroom where she repeats her confession "of her own free will and accord." If she changes her mind, it was back to the torture chamber for some more pain. The outcome of the whole thing is an execution, although some soft-hearted judges merely took away all of the victim's property and forced her to wear a yellow cross sewn on her clothing—for the rest of her life.

Of course, America had its witch problems, too, although the witch hunt did not last as long here as it did across the Atlantic. There had been instances of reported witchcraft in the American Colonies even before 1650, but the full-scale witch hunt seemed to begin about 1688.

A Boston mason, John Goodwin, had hired an Irish washerwoman named Glover. Soon afterwards, Goodwin's children began to have fits and utter blasphemies. "Witch" Glover was accused of causing this strange behavior and was hanged. It was later suggested that the only spell she uttered was the saying of her Rosary in Gaelic.

Cotton Mather, a minister and former teacher at Harvard was preaching at Boston's North Church. He was curious about the behavior of Goodwin's four children, who, by the way, were still having fits after the hanging. Mather took the oldest child, Martha, home with him, and made a thorough study of her sickness.

Through the study of Martha and his own observations, Mather then published a book about his studies, called *Late Memorable Providences Relating to Witchcraft and Possession.* This book was widely read and widely believed, and was one of the causes of the explosive witch hunt that began to infest the colonies.

The witch hunt spread through the British colonies of Massachusetts, Connecticut and as far north as Maine. But probably the most famous outbreak was in Salem, Massachusetts. As the story is recorded, it all began in 1692 in the home of the Reverend Parris, who had just recently arrived to become the minister of the church in Salem Village.

He had brought with him two black slaves that he had acquired while he was in the Barbados, a woman named Tituba and a man called John Indian. The Parrises' nine-year-old daughter, Elizabeth, began almost immediately to make friends with the young girls of the town. These girls also grew attached to Tituba, who would entertain them by teaching them about fortune telling.

One winter evening, the group of girls was seated in the kitchen of the parsonage listening to Tituba's tales. The girls, getting more and more excited, began laughing and crying and seemed to be having fits. Mrs. Parris, naturally, became quite concerned, and told her husband about what was happening in the kitchen. It so happened that Mr. Parris was particularly worried about the stories of witchcraft that were then traveling all over the Colony of Massachusetts, and he sent for a doctor. When the doctor arrived he found the girls groaning and growling. Some of them went down on all fours and tried to bite him on the ankle. The doctor announced that they were bewitched.

When Parris confronted the girls and asked them if they were bewitched, they said that they were. They also named three people, who, they said, had caused the whole thing. On February 29, 1692, warrants were issued for the arrest of the three on charges of witchcraft. One of them was Sarah Good, a shrewish hag who begged for food. Another was Sarah Osburn, an invalid. The third was Tituba. Thus began the terror that eventually led to some twenty deaths and the jailing of about one hundred and fifty people.

The trial was held by Magistrate Corwin. Sarah Good was convicted of the charges and hanged. Sarah Osburn died in jail. Tituba, who confessed, was imprisoned for over a year and then sold as a slave.

While the witch hunt went on in Salem, homes of those accused of witchcraft were seized and the sheriff and his men divided up all of the furniture and livestock and kept it. The accused people had to pay for their own food and fuel while in jail, and they even had to pay for the chains that were used to tie them up. If they couldn't pay, their children were billed for the expenses. According to legal records of that time, these practices were not uncommon. In addition, other fees were also charged—there were even fees to pay for the hangman and fees to be paid by the family in order to retrieve the body of the executed witch.

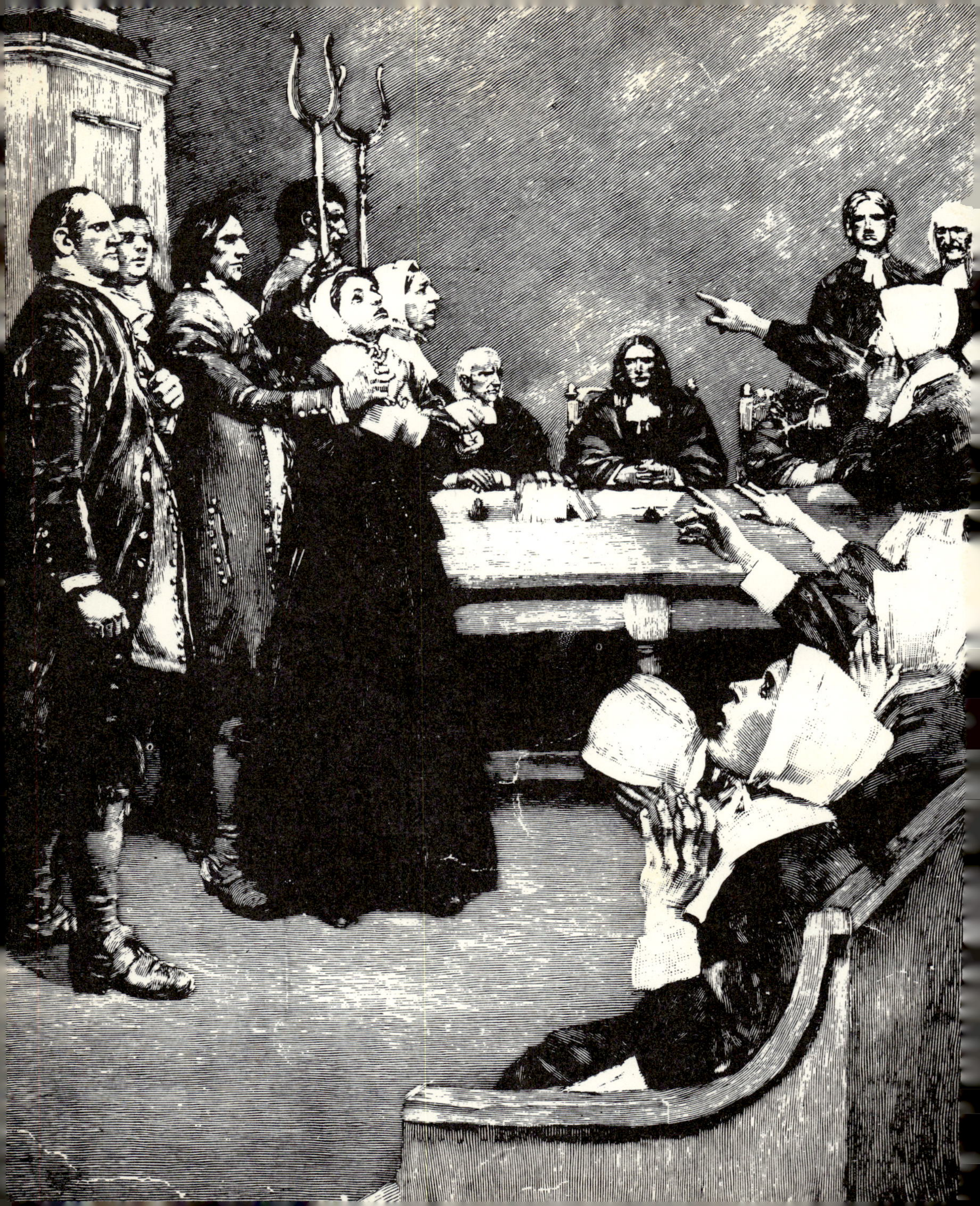

A Salem witch trial. The pointing girls are accusing the victim by screaming, "There is a flock of yellow birds around her head!"

One of the Salem witch trials was that of Rebekah Nurse, who was accused by a twelve-year-old girl and her mother, as well as by an eleven-year-old girl. The story of this trial was written by Parris, who said that the three witnesses fell into fits and swore that evil spirits (which only they could see) had entered the courtroom. They also claimed to see the Devil whispering in Mrs. Nurse's ear, and that strange birds were flying around her head.

They said that the accused had murdered six children; the witnesses saw this, they said, in their dreams. Even though more than twenty outstanding citizens of Salem testified in favor of Mrs. Nurse, she was found guilty, she was excommunicated from the church, and then she was hanged. Several years later, the First Church of Salem repealed the excommunication, but it was too late.

Several other people were executed in Salem, one of them a former minister of Ipswich named George Burroughs. The ghosts of his former two wives had appeared in a vision of a young child and accused Burroughs of murdering them. This was enough evidence to bring him back from Maine, where he was then living, for trial. A man named John Willard was employed to arrest witches, but when he saw what happened to his prisoners, he refused to continue in his work. So he was executed too. Even dogs were accused of being familiars and were executed.

The Salem witch hunt, and in fact, the witch hunts all over the colonies ended as suddenly as they had begun. The people in Salem became disillusioned from the needless executions and pressure was exerted by the Massachusetts governor. They even rejected their minister, Mr. Parris, and in one instance withheld his salary. Most of the people who had participated in the trials made public apologies, while many jurors apologized in writing.

Judge Sewall, one of the well-known hanging judges, went to Sunday services one day in the Old South Church in Boston, and rose up before the congregation. He handed a written confession to the minister of that church, signifying his sin and repentance. Not only that, but he also remained standing while it was read aloud. Then he begged the congregation to pray for him. It is said that, as long as he lived, he spent one day each year in prayer and fasting.

In 1697, the town of Salem set aside January 16 as a day of public fast and repentance. Later, a number of the children of executed "witches" demanded the return of the stolen property and a public proclamation that their parents had not been witches. The convictions of their parents were reversed; 597 pounds and 12 shillings was divided among the children.

Some of the witches, of course, had had no children, and so six of these unfortunates were still, in the eyes of the law, guilty of witchcraft. But in the 1950's, Vance Greenslit, a relative of Ann Pudeator, one of the witches, petitioned to have the names of the remaining six cleared.

At first, the Massachusetts Legislature refused. After all, it said, Massachusetts was not responsible, since Salem was in a British colony at the time of the trials. The Parliament in London would have to make amends. But the British Parliament had already refused to take this action. Finally, the repentant Massachusetts Legislature reversed the convictions of the six in 1957. But this was done only after a decree that no damages in the form of money or property could be paid to the descendents of the six.

Perhaps the days of the witch hunt are not over. In February of 1969, two Swiss religious leaders were sentenced to ten years in prison for beating an accused witch to death. Bernadette Hasler, a seventeen-year-old girl, had been flogged for over an hour to drive the Devil out of her.

The following page shows informers, at a Salem witch trial, swearing that their neighbors were witches.

SEVEN / THE BLACK MASS / There is a great deal of argument concerning the Black Mass. Some historians say that this was a regular happening at the witches' Sabbats, while others say that it never happened at all. The truth is probably somewhere in between these two points of view.

The Black Mass is supposed to be a ceremony that mocks the communion service of the Christian churches. It is complete with such little twists as reciting the Lord's Prayer backwards, having the Devil give a sermon that praises evil, and many more touches of disrespect, heresy, and blasphemy.

There was a case in which Pierre Aupetit, a French clergyman, was burned at the stake for supposedly organizing one of these ceremonies. In his Black Mass, it was confessed, the Devil gave the sermon. And when it came time to consecrate the host, all of the witches who were present muttered, "Beelzebub, Beelzebub, Beelzebub," instead of "Father, Son, and Holy Spirit." The Devil took the form of a butterfly, and all of the members of the congregation were then given black wafers—representing the host—which they were instructed to chew up thoroughly before they swallowed them.

A reasonable point of view about the popularity of the Black Mass can be described like this. There were a few cases of this ceremony during the period of 1300 to 1600. But the uproar against witches as heretics was so wild at the time that the reports of Black Masses were more numerous than the actual happenings. It would seem that the idea of the desecration of the host enflamed those people who were accusing others of being witches.

During the 1700's, some bored, upper-class people held Black Masses—not because they actually believed in witchcraft, but just because they did not have much else to do to entertain themselves. It wasn't until the 1800's, after the witch hysteria had died out, that the Black Mass really came into its own. But again, most of the people celebrating the Black Mass did not believe themselves to be witches. They were probably just fooling around. So, the more recent Black Masses did not grow out of witchcraft; they were merely performed by people who had read about witchcraft.

However, we cannot deny that the Black Mass itself is considered by most people to be heretical and blasphemous. It is a way of worshipping the Devil, even though the witches of the Middle Ages did not seem to use it too much.

Since one of the main parts of the Christian mass is the swallowing of the host—the consecrated wafer—the practitioners of the Black Mass thought up quite a variety of substitutes for this item. Since the wafer is white, most of these desecrations were either black or were colored black by the celebrants. Sometimes a turnip stained black was used. On other occasions, black bread was consecrated in the Devil's name. If the congregation happened to be wealthy, they might have special wafers made with a picture of the Devil on them.

Another trick was often used. The Devil worshippers would go to a real mass, take the wafer, conceal it, and leave the church. This trick was also used by those early witches who were looking for their familiars, you will remember. The heretics might even go to all the trouble of putting alum in their mouths so that their mouths would be so dry that the wafer would not disintegrate. It would then be saved and used as the blasphemous host in some Black Mass or other ceremony.

So much for the basic equipment. The Black Mass is ready to begin. Ideally, the service is conducted by an unfrocked priest. A girl without clothes lies on the altar and a crucifix is hung over her, upside-down. The regular mass is said backwards, perhaps almost word-for-word, with two exceptions. Whenever the word "God" appears, the priest says "Satan," and whenever the word "good" comes along, the word "evil" is substituted. So now the whole mass has become topsy-turvy.

Then wine from a chalice is usually spilled over the girl on the altar. Disgusting mixtures, even human blood, may be substituted for the sacramental wine or the holy water of the legitimate mass.

One of the weirdest descriptions of a Black Mass tells of a meeting in a ruined church at midnight. The unfrocked priest wears black vestments and carries black candles. The holy water has previously been used to drown an unbaptized new-born baby. The altar is decorated with owls, bats, and toads, instead of flowers. The service ends with the desecration of a crucifix, which is not only stamped upon, but spit upon.

As was mentioned, although there is some evidence that these obscene rites were practiced during the Middle Ages, they really seemed to catch on with people who were looking for a new thrill in the eighteenth century. Some of these belonged to the famous Hellfire Club in London. There were also similar clubs in other parts of England, Ireland, and Scotland. In the nineteenth century, the Black

Mass was celebrated by a group of students at Oxford University. Another group popped up at Oxford in 1912, and yet another in London in 1934.

Some students of the Black Mass have told of ceremonies in such places as Lyons (France), New York, and Paris. There is convincing proof that these rites are happening in our own time. In 1963, a Black Mass was reported to have been said in Bedfordshire, England, in which the bones of a woman—stolen from a grave—were laid out on the church floor and a strange cross was drawn in red on the walls of the church. Thirteen "worshippers" repeated the Lord's Prayer backwards, ate stolen communion wafers, and sacrificed a rooster on the altar.

In that same year, Princess Irene of Greece, the wife of a famous anthropologist, wrote a magazine article telling of a Black Mass that she had seen in Paris. In 1964, a Scottish Presbyterian minister found a torn-up Bible, a broken chalice, and an upside-down cross in a ruined seventeenth century church.

Actually, the Black Mass is primarily a modern invention, and it seems to be practiced by small groups all over the civilized world today. Indeed, there are groups of witches all over the world right now carrying out their ceremonies, casting spells, and generally having a wild time. But few people seem to care. Witches today are seldom arrested, except for disturbing the peace.

In the United States, most of the individual states have repealed their old laws against witchcraft. France has done the same. England cancelled its bans in 1951. And in Germany, during the 1950's, a campaign of education was begun to reduce the numbers of witches in the rural areas. But most of the witches practicing today are members of the group, a seemingly modern invention, called the "white witches."

EIGHT / WHITE WITCHES / Modern witches are usually organized into groups called covens. These covens consist of thirteen members each—twelve witches and their officer.

There are those who think that even witches of the Middle Ages were organized into these groups. There was a mention of a coven in a witch trial in 1567, and a few other covens were reported during the next few centuries. The coven would meet, perhaps at an Esbat, to compare notes on witchcraft, practice magic, and get orders from the leader.

Although there is some doubt that witches of the past formed themselves into covens, there is no doubt that our twentieth-century witches often meet in groups of thirteen. By the way, the number thirteen may be a grim joke about the twelve apostles and Christ. That was a group of thirteen, too. At any rate, the story of modern witchcraft does include the coven.

Great Britain seems to be a hotbed of witches' covens. Estimates of the numbers of witches in the British Isles range from four hundred to five thousand, depending on who does the estimating, and there is a plan on foot to organize them all into Witches Incorporated, with headquarters in London. But there are also covens in the United States and other countries, who carry on in more secrecy than their brothers and sisters in Great Britain.

It is very difficult these days for intelligent people to believe in the Devil—at least as a living, breathing organism who is the cause of all evil thoughts and evil deeds. Even our modern witches have rejected the idea of Devil worship, to concentrate on the practice of magic. They work on charms, such as mixing the ashes of a toad with brandy to cure drunkenness. They try out home remedies, such as hanging a mouse's tooth around a baby's neck to ease the baby's teething pains. There is a certain amount of unusual worship at coven meetings; however, it is the worship of strange, but non-evil, gods. The religious part of a coven meeting always seems to include dancing naked around a fire.

Modern witches worship several different gods. Probably the most important one is the Great Mother, or Earth Mother, who is the goddess of fertility. She is also called Cybele, Demeter, the Mountain Mother, Isis, Astarte, Ishtar, Artemis, Diana, Venus, and Aphrodite, depending on which system of mythology the coven is partial to. They may also worship a male god of good power, not evil power, called the Horned God, or sometimes Pan.

If there is no connection between modern witches and the witches of the Middle Ages, there may be one between the witch of today and some others of antiquity. There are ancient Scandinavian legends of women who could fly and metamorphose. A Mexican group (before Columbus) had meetings similar to Sabbats at which a priestess was the leader. The Egyptians and Greeks had fertility ceremonies. But all of these witches of the past were, as are witches of today, believers in white magic.

The coven of today may meet once a week, or only on the evenings before the first day of each new season of the year. Of the thirteen members of the coven, there are six male witches, six female witches, and a leader. This leader may sometimes be a man, but is more often a woman, called the High Priestess.

The meetings are most often held in the living room of a member of the coven's home, although, if the weather is nice, the group may meet outdoors. Once in a while, a wealthy coven can afford to set up a special room that is used only for the meetings.

The first thing to do is to draw a chalk circle on the floor, nine feet across. Then this circle is retraced with a magic witch knife, called an athame. The next step in the order of business is to have all the witches remove their clothing.

Accounts acknowledge that the purpose of the circle is the direct opposite from the purpose of the evil magician when he draws a circle. The evil magician draws it to stand in and thus protect himself from the evil demons that he summons up from the Underworld. The white witches draw the circle—not to keep spirits out of it—but rather to keep the magic inside of it. They remove their clothing because they believe that their power comes from their own bodies, and clothing can prevent this magical power from being effective.

Few details of the ceremonies of white witches are available. We know that incense is used. We know that water and salt (that substance so horrible and sickening to the evil witch) are consecrated. We know that all of the witches must be purified before the ceremony can be started.

The High Priestess calls for the god or the goddess or both. Then all of the members of the coven hold up their knives and worship these deities. If the meeting is held outside, there may be a fire in the center of the circle. The priestess may read from a collection of ancient writings, called *The Book of Shadows.* Then the members join hands, dance around the circle, and begin to sing. The whole thing is followed by a grand feast, and the meeting is adjourned. Not much has happened, but everyone is satisfied and goes away happy.

As it stands now, our modern witches have given up on all of the old black magic stuff. They don't use skulls or stick pins in dolls. They don't have devil-masks, or ride broomsticks. And they don't make sacrifices. Not only that, but they do not mock the Christian religion by holding Black Masses. Probably the only frightening thing about them is the use of the athame.

NINE / SCIENCE AND WITCHCRAFT /

If we want to look at the story of witchcraft in the western world through the eyes of the modern scientist, we must really go back to the beginnings of the persecution of witches. Let's set the stage. Here is the situation, long, long ago.

To begin with, ever since the dawn of time, men have believed in magic. One jump away from magic was black magic. And one step away from that was witchcraft. The concern about witchcraft that led to the witch hunts seems to have started in Spain, jumped to France, moved to Paris, then to Italy, then to what is now Germany, and finally to Britain and her overseas colonies in America.

People all over the western Christian world began to believe in witches who worshipped the Devil and performed black magic. In the middle of the night, at the dawn, at sunset, and even at high noon, the forces of evil were at work, people believed. There could be evil spirits in a stream, a lake, or a forest, lying in wait to commit mayhem on an unsuspecting traveler.

Evil forces were everywhere.
Even with the family
and clergymen nearby,
a man, in his own home,
in his own bed,
could be tempted by demons.

Some believed there were horrible spirits in the church graveyard or on the spot where thieves were hanged, or maybe there were demons in swamps, in marshes, and in caves. Even the mountain slopes and summits were peopled by messengers of the Devil. Everywhere you looked, evil forces could be hiding.

At night, there were ill winds blowing up from Hell. Incubi and succubi hung around God-fearing people's houses to bring madness and dishonor to a man and his wife and his children. The moon and the stars cast an evil magical light on all righteous persons. Any piece of meat or any drink of water might just possibly have been enchanted by a witch.

The person who laughed too much might be bewitched. The person who appreciated beauty too much might be bewitched. The person who walked in his sleep might be bewitched. The person who was dull-witted or ugly might be bewitched. In short, anyone who was not quite the same as his neighbors might be bewitched.

No wonder that thousands of people believed in witchcraft. No wonder, also, that many people thought that they could protect themselves by joining the witches and becoming a part of the group who worshipped the Devil. So, if we keep in mind that these folk believed in witchcraft, we can easily see that it is a short step from this belief to certain pathological states of mind.

It is likely that the whole business of obsession and possession can be explained away by psychologists or psychiatrists. After all, obsession is merely a state of mind in which the patient has a fixed idea that is not normal. He might only fear that everyone is out to get him, but he might also fear that he is being attacked by demons. This sounds remarkably like a mental illness called paranoia. We know that obsession can be caused by a great shock, weakened will power, or even by poor health. This means that the witch-fearers of the Middle Ages were in a proper frame of mind to believe that they were obsessed, although they might only have been mentally ill.

In the case of possession, a demon is supposedly occupying the body of the victim. Many times, possession was used as an excuse by a wrong-doer to explain away his or her sins. But there is a psychological explanation for the cases of those who honestly thought that they were possessed. They may have been suffering from schizophrenia. This is a disease in which the patient loses contact with reality. He also may lose his own personality to such an extent that he may think that he is really, at times, another person. What a subject for burning the schizophrenic would make—if we believed in witchcraft.

So the situation was simple. Put together a few people who believed they were witches, and add a vast number of people who, although honest, were suffering from hysteria. Mix in the idea held by many authorities that witches were adept at hypnotism and extra-sensory perception. What do we end up with? An atmosphere all over the western world that made the time ripe for the witch hunts.

We can also learn something by examining the witches' use of chemicals. The most prominent mixtures were those that were used for the preparation of flying ointments. Basically, there were three recipes:

1. Parsley, water of aconite, poplar leaves, and soot.
2. Water parsnip, sweet flag, cinquefoil, bat's blood, deadly nightshade, and oil.
3. Baby's fat, juice of water parsnip, aconite, cinquefoil, deadly nightshade, and soot.

Now, aconite and deadly nightshade (belladonna) are two of the three most poisonous plants to be found in Europe. The third is hemlock, and there is a possibility that the parsley of the formula is hemlock, and not the garnish that we all know so well. Aconite produces a slowing down of the heartbeat, and belladonna produces a wild excitement and delirious dreams. Hemlock acts in the same way as belladonna.

So the concoction in recipe number one would produce a mental confusion, slowed-down movements, irregular heartbeats, dizziness, and shortness of breath. The second recipe would produce excitement leading into delirium. The third causes excitement and irregular heart action. Anyone who used these ointments might well be a candidate for the belief that she was flying to a witches' Sabbat.

Let's pretend, although it was not always true, that those who honestly believed themselves to be witches were really mentally ill. What has been the history of their treatment? Actually, man's understanding of the mentally ill has always been incomplete. He has, at times, thought that demons should be exorcised from the patient, or that the patient should be punished by society. Even today there is often a stigma attached to the person who has, or has had, a mental disease.

In the days of ancient Greece, the mental patient was "cured" by immersion in oil or water. He also might be given enemas, strong drink, or even excessive lovemaking. But by the beginning of the Christian era, he was much more likely to be punished than treated. At this time, he might be starved, chained, or flogged. This seemed to be the fashion for hundreds of years, for in 1845 a speech was made in the British House of Commons that recommended as the only approved remedies for madness, "chains, whips, darkness, and solitude."

But during the Middle Ages, with the rise of Devil worship, came epidemics of flagellation (whipping), wild dancing, and demonic possession. The church and the congregations used incantations, charms, and spells against this. Then came the witch hunt. Those who were mentally ill were treated as wild animals. They were chained. They were beaten. They were tortured. And they were executed.

John Weyer, as mentioned before, led the way toward the humane treatment of the mentally ill, but he was largely ignored. It was not until 1792, when much of the witch hysteria had disappeared, that a French physician, Phillipe Pinel, made a giant step toward curing the mentally ill. He released fifty-three of his mental patients from their chains. Then came a new day in psychiatry. The whip was replaced by education, recreation, socially-useful work, and drugs.

In the 1800's, it was found that there was hope for a cure for many of these diseases—even as high as from eighty to ninety per cent of them. But this enthusiasm died soon afterwards. Back came the cruelty. Insane asylums became overcrowded, budgets became tight, personnel were not trained properly, and little that was new happened until the middle of the 1900's.

Since that time, many things have been tried. Hypnosis, rest cures, psychotherapy, shock treatment, lobotomies, drug therapy—all had their moment in the sun. But most of them were found to have quite disturbing side-effects.

Today, our treatment of the mentally disturbed seems to have settled in the movement of community psychiatry. Patients remain in their own towns, go to clinics and hospital units for treatment, and then return home. But if this is to become successful, people are going to have to change their attitudes toward the mental patient. It will be an uphill fight, and the end is not in sight. Not only that, but also we may find out that our system of treatments has been wrong once again.

However, one thing is sure. There will never be another period like that of the witch hunts with its hysterical persecutions and tortures and executions.

Or will there. . . . .?

ACKNOWLEDGEMENTS/ My sincere thanks to E. John and Nancy DeWaard and to Fr. Norman F. Catir, Jr., for letting me raid their libraries; and to Ray Broekel, whose idea this whole thing was.

Illustrations

The following are from the New York Public Library photo collections:

page 8: from *Newes from Scotland*, 1591
pages 14–15: ancient copy of a woodcut by Holbein, taken from the German translation of Boethius' *De Consolatione Philisophiae*, Augsburg edition, 1537
page 25: original source unknown
pages: 26, 60–61, 68–69, from *Historia de gentibus septentrionalibus*, by Olaus Magnus, Rome, 1555
pages 29, 30: from the *Compendium Maleficarum*, by Guazzo, 1626
page 35: from altarpiece in the Cologne Museum
page 36: picture by Michael Pacher
page 39: original source unknown
pages 48–49: Composed by Bruegel the Elder, engraved by Cock in the 16th century
page 53: ancient woodcut
page 70: original source unknown
page 87: ancient woodcut
page 88: ancient woodcut
pages 94, 98–99: from *Harper's Magazine*, 1892
page 113: original source unknown, woodcut dated 1497

Chapter Symbols

Chapter symbols were taken from *Symbols, Signs, and Signets* by Ernst Lehner, World Publishing Company, 1950

page 11: Chapter One, an Egyptian symbol, p. 82, Fig. 417, meaning *Life*
page 23: Chapter Two, one of the magic seals of the three princes of the world of spirits, p. 103, Fig. 569, meaning *Lucifer*
page 45: Chapter Three, Ibid., Fig. 570, meaning *Beelzebub*
page 62: Chapter Four, Ibid., Fig. 571, meaning *Satan*
page 71: Chapter Five, Ibid., Fig. 572, meaning *Astoroth*
page 83: Chapter Six, Ibid., Fig. 573, meaning *Leviathan*
page 100: Chapter Seven, Ibid., Fig. 574, meaning *Elimi*
page 106: Chapter Eight, Ibid., Fig. 575, meaning *Baalbarith*
page 111: Chapter Nine, a Nordic rune, p. 99, Fig. 534, meaning *Against Witchcraft*

INDEX

A

Athame, 108, 110
Abbé Adams, 37–38
"Agia", 81–82
Anglican Church, 42–43

B

Binsfeld, Peter, Bishop of Treres, 17
Black Magicians, 21
Black Mass, 100–105
  England, 103–105
  France, 100–101, 105
  U.S.A., 104–105
Book of Death, 30
"Book of Shadows", 109
Brothers Grimm, 12
Burroughs, George, 95–96

C

Cambions, 33
Ceremonies and feasts, 45–59
Chemicals, 74, 81, 102, 115–116
Christianity, 13, 21, 28–30, 46, 56, 64, 83, 100–103, 111, 116
Convictions, 84–99
Covenant, 31–32
Covens, 106–109

D

Dances, 57–59
Demons, 19, 33–44, 54, 84, 114
Devil, 12–13, 16, 18–19, 22–33, 40, 43, 54–59, 62–67, 73, 75–76, 78–81, 100–102, 107, 111–114, 117
"Devil's horn", 80
"Devil's mark", 30–31, 75, 86

E

Eastern Orthodox Church, 43
Enchantment, 72
Encyclopedia of Occultism, 40
Esbat, 59, 78, 90
Evil eye, 71–72, 81
Exorcising, 42–44

F

Familiars, 74–78, 85–86, 96
Father Spee, 19
Fertility, 66–67, 107
Flying, 51–52, 74
Fumigation, 42

G

Gaufridi, Louis, 32
Good, Sarah, 93
Goodwin, John, 91
Greenslit, Vance, 97

H

Hansel and Gretel, 12
Hasler, Bernadette, 97
Heretics, 83
Hex, 57
High Priestess, 108–109

I

Incubus, 32–33
Inquisition, 20, 84, 89
Insistor, Henricus, 84

J

Jewish festivals, 45–46
Judge Sewall, 96

K

Knights Templar, 84

L

Late Memorable Providences Relating to Witchcraft and Possession, 91–92
Legislature, Massachusetts, 97
Lutheran Church, 44

M

Macbeth, 11
Magician, 20–21
Malleus Maleficarum, 84
Mather, Cotton, 91
Meeting-places, 52, 54
Metamorphosis, 73–74
Middle Ages, 13, 16, 45, 64, 72, 102–103, 106, 108, 114, 117

N

Newton, Florence, 72
Nurse, Rebekah, 95

O

Obsession, 34–39, 114
Ointments, magic, 51, 54
Old South Church, Boston, 96
Osburn, Sarah, 93
Osculum infame, 55

P

Parris, Reverend, 92–93, 95, 96
Pinel, Phillipe, 117
Pope Innocent IV, 85
Pope Innocent VIII, 66
Possession, 33–34, 38, 40–42, 114
Predictions, 50
"Pricking", 86–88
Protestant Reformation, 43–44
Prudeator, Ann, 97

R

Remy, Nicholas, 16
Roman Catholic Church, 43

S

Sabbat, 45–59, 74, 78, 90, 100, 108, 116
Sacrifice, 56, 62–67, 110
Salem, Massachusetts, 54, 92–97
Satan, see Devil
Schizophrenic, 42, 114–115
Science and witchcraft, 111–118
Scott, Reginald, 19
Sorcerer; sorceress, 21
Spells, 73–74, 77–82
Sprenger, Jacob, 84
St. Anthony, 34, 36–37
Succubus, 32–33

T

Tituba, 92–93
Tortures, 85–91, 97, 116–117
Trials, 84–85, 89–90, 93–97

U

United Church of Christ, 44

W

Walpurgis Night, 47
Warlock, 20
West, William, 12
Weyer, John, 18–19, 117
White magic, 21
White witches, 21, 105–110
Willard, John, 96
Wier, Jan, see John Weyer

Witch
  description, 12–13
  definition, 20–22
"Witch" Glover, 91
Witch hunting, 83–97, 117
Witch power, 71–82
Witch, white, 21, 105–110
Witchcraft, history of, 11–22
Witches Sabbath, 45
"Witch's mark", 75, 86
Wizard, 20
Wizard of Oz, 11

ABOUT THE AUTHOR/A curiosity for the unexplained and an infectious interest in the unknown—especially when writing about the supernatural—seem to be inherent qualities of the author When Thomas G. Aylesworth combines his scientific background with a comprehensive study of the mysterious, the reader enters a world of witchcraft and necromancy.

Since earning his Ph.D. from Ohio State University, he has been an assistant professor at Michigan State University, and Senior Editor of Current Science. Presently, Dr. Aylesworth is Senior Editor at Doubleday and Company and The Natural History Press.

The author of eight books since 1964, a member of the New York Academy of Science, Phi Delta Kappa, the National Association of Biology Teachers, and the Central Association of Science and Math Teachers, Dr. Aylesworth still finds time for sailing or playing tennis. As a matter of fact, he prefers listening to music over the practical application of the occult.